I0698626

Industries That Can Make You A Millionaire

The ultimate eye-opener on business and industries that can make you a millionaire in few years

Prof. Michael Banks

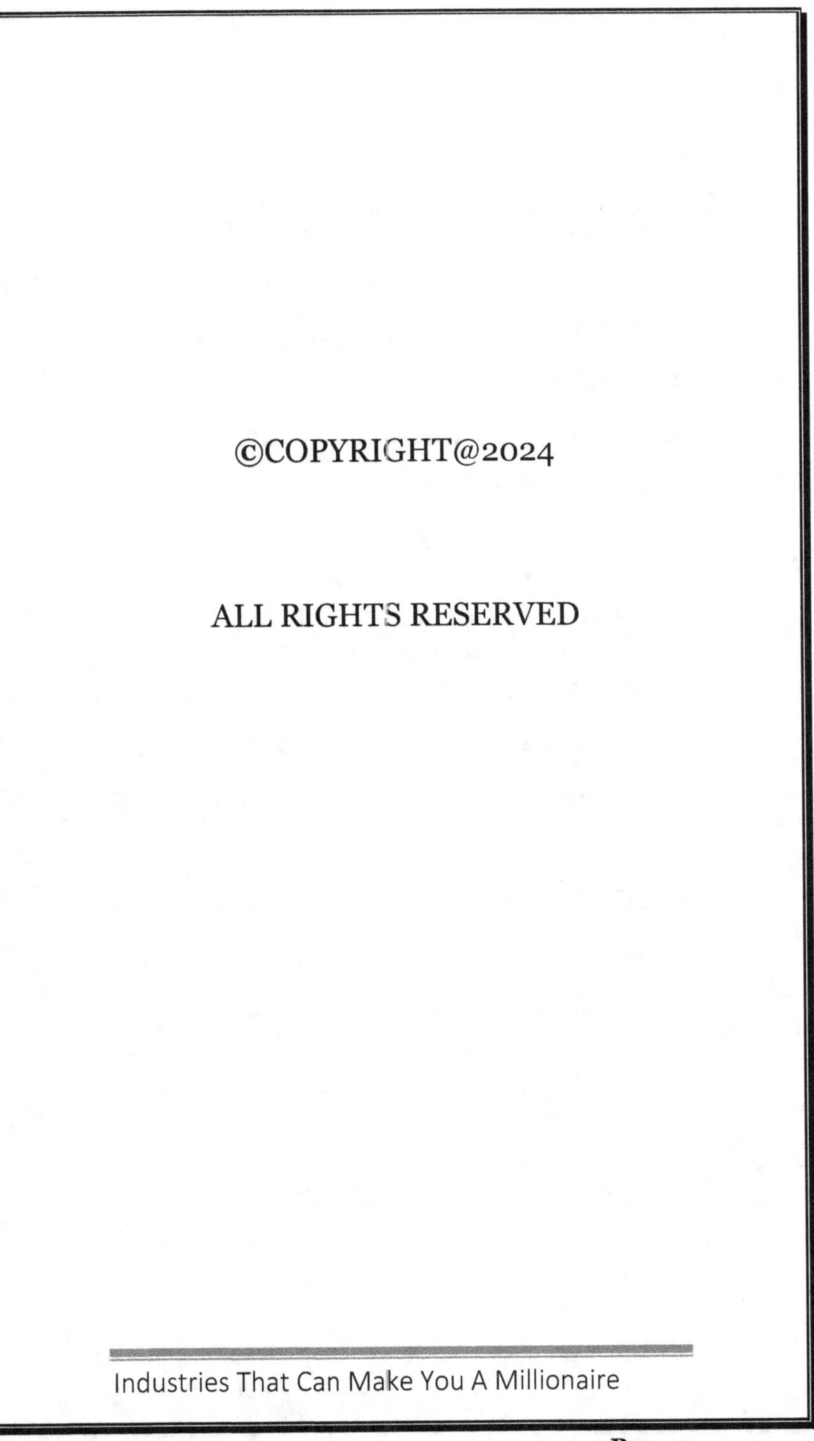

Industries That Can Make You A Millionaire

TABLE OF CONTENT

FORWARD

This book is precisely a material for a basic overview on multimillion dollars businesses. However, note that this book does not have complete guide on how to start these business.

Should in case you pick interest in any of the industry to invest in, check out my specific books on each of these businesses as that is where you will find detailed information, step by step guide on how to start each of the businesses, basic rules engaging the industries etc.

Introduction

I've never met any individual who would rather not earn more money; in any event, when they pretend about it, their actions often give them away. You wanted that advanced education so you can have the opportunity to bring in more money from your work. You look for grants (scholarship) to have the option to get quality schooling with another person paying the cash. Your parents believed you should go to class, get good grades and find a decent line of work so you can take in substantial income and carry on with a superior life. The world framework (system) is built around money. Therefore, the individuals who attempt to deny this frequently fall victim to the system.

So what are the absolute most effective ways to situate yourself to earn more cash? You can either decide to indiscriminately seek after a career in prehistory or search for where there is a more prominent chance to make wealth and riches. Most times, the most ideal way to distinguish opportunities is to follow the money. You pose the inquiry which industry has created the most wealth? Which ventures are the quickest developing? Responding to questions like these can direct you perfectly positioned toward the right place to develop your fundamental interest and energy.

On account of certain industries, every business visionary (entrepreneur) has the chance to develop and arrive at the million-dollar mark. You can quit living in the red and win the best way of life you want.

The monetary industry, for example, has made the most tycoons, as indicated by the Wealth Report. The tech industry, insurance, and medical services are ways of developing riches and accomplish more through careers or entrepreneurship.

Chapter 1
Oil and Gas Industry

The oil and gas industry is perhaps the biggest area on the planet in terms of dollar value, producing an expected $5 trillion in worldwide income as of 2023.

Oil is pivotal to the global monetary structure, affecting everything from transportation to heating and electricity to industrial production and manufacturing.

Investors who are hoping to enter the oil and gas industry can rapidly be overpowered by the intricate language and exceptional measurements utilized all through the area. This brief is designed to provide assistance to anybody who wants to comprehend or understand the fundamentals of organizations engaged with the oil and gas sector by explaining the concept of key ideas and the guidelines of estimation and measurements.

Note;

- The oil and gas industry is separated into three fragments: upstream, midstream, and downstream.
- Upstream, or exploration and production (E&P) organizations, find reservoirs and drill oil and gas wells.

- Midstream companies are answerable for transportation from the wells to refineries.
- Downstream companies are responsible for refining and the offer of the completed products.
- Drilling companies contract their administrations to E&P companies to extract oil and gas.
- Well-servicing companies conduct related development and maintenance exercises on well sites.

So What Is Oil and Gas Production?

Oil and gas creation is a multi-stage whole process of discovering an asset, transporting it to a processing plant (refinery) and transforming it into a completed item prepared and available to be purchased. Or then again, in industry terminology, upstream, midstream, and downstream sections.

- **About Hydrocarbons**

Hydrocarbons make up unrefined petroleum and natural gas, which are normally happening substances tracked down in rock in the earth's crust. These natural unrefined components are made by the compression of the remains of plants and animals in sedimentary rocks like sandstone, limestone, and shale.

The sedimentary stone itself is a result of stores in Old Ocean and different water bodies. As layers of silt were saved on the ocean floor, the decaying remains from plants and animals were coordinated into the forming rock. The organic material at last changes into oil and gas in the wake of being exposed to specific temperatures and pressure inside the earth's crust.

Oil and gas are less dense than water, so they move through permeable sedimentary rock toward the earth's crust. At the point when the hydrocarbons are trapped underneath less-permeable cap rock, an oil and gas reservoir is framed. These reservoirs of oil and gas represent our source of raw petroleum and natural gas.

Hydrocarbons are brought to the surface by boring (drilling) through the cap rock and into the reservoir. When the bore reaches the reservoir, a useful oil or gas well can be constructed and the hydrocarbons can be syphoned (pumped) to the surface. While the drilling action doesn't find industrially practical amounts of plugged, the well is named a dry hole, which is typically stopped and deserted.

Hydrocarbons trapped in rock formation, for example, oil shale can be extracted by infusing high-pressure liquid into the ground and fracturing the stone, a cycle known as "deep oil drilling."

Upstream, Midstream, Downstream

The oil and gas industry is broken down into three main parts: **upstream, midstream, and downstream.**

Upstream

Upstream businesses are organizations associated with the investigation (exploration) and creation of oil and gas. These are the organizations that scan the world for repositories (reservoirs) of the unrefined material and afterward drill to extract that material. These firms are frequently known as "E&P" for "exploration and Production."

The upstream section is characterized by high-risk, high investment capital, extended duration as it requires Time to locate and drill, as well as being technologically intensive. Essentially all income and pay proclamation details of E&P companies are straightforwardly connected with oil and gas production.

E&P organizations don't normally own their own drilling tools or employ a drilling rig staff. Instead, they hire contract drilling organizations to drill wells for themselves and the contract drilling organizations by and large charge for their services in view of how much time they work for an E&P organization.

Drillers don't create income that is tied straightforwardly to oil and gas creation, just like the case for E&P organizations. When a well is bored (drilled), different activities are engaged with creating and managing up with its production after time. These activities are called well adjusting and can incorporate logging, cementing, casing, puncturing, fracturing, and maintenance. Oil drilling and oil servicing in this way address two distinct business activities inside the oil and gas industry.

Midstream

Midstream businesses are those that are centered on transportation. They are the ones responsible for moving the extracted unrefined materials to the refinery to process the oil and gas. Midstream companies are characterized by transportation, shipping, pipelines, and storing natural substances (raw materials).

The midstream section is additionally set apart by high guidelines, especially on pipeline transmission, and low capital risk. The section is likewise normally reliant upon the success and outcome of upstream firms.

Downstream

Downstream businesses are the processing plants (refineries) and gas sections. Processing plants (refineries) are the companies responsible for eliminating pollution (impurity) and changing the oil and gas completely to products for the general public, like gasoline, jet fuel, heating oil, and black-top (asphalt). Gas stations are where buyers fuel up at the pump.

Understanding Oil Production Numbers

E&P (exploration and production) organizations measure oil production in barrels. One barrel, usually curtailed as BBL, is equivalent to 42 U.S. gallons. Companies frequently describe Production BBL each day or BBL per quarter.

A typical procedure in the oil patch is to use a prefix of "M" to show 1,000 and a prefix of "MM" to show 1 million. Subsequently, 1,000 barrels are generally signified as MBBL, and 1 million barrels are meant as MMBBL. For instance, when an E&P company reports production of seven MBBL each day, it implies 7,000 barrels of oil each day.

Similar to the case for drilling, numerous public organizations are engaged with well service activity. The income of service organizations is attached to the activity level in the oil and gas industry. Rig count and use rates are marks or indicators of how much activity occurs in the US at any given time.

Understanding Gas Production Numbers

Flammable gas (natural gas) production is portrayed in terms of cubic feet. Like the conversation for oil, the term MMCF implies 1 million cubic feet of gas. BCF implies 1 billion cubic feet and TCF describes 1 trillion cubic feet.

Note that flammable gas (natural gas) trades on the CME group (The Chicago Mercantile Exchange) future exchange, however are not estimated in cubic feet. All things considered, the future contract depends on 1 million English thermal units, or MMBtu, which is generally identical to 970 cubic feet of gas.

E&P companies frequently depict their Production in units of Barrels of Oil Equivalent (BOE). To ascertain or calculate BOE, companies usually convert gas production into oil equivalent production. In this estimation, one BOE has what could be compared to 6,040 cubic feet of gas or approximately one BBL to six Mcf.

Oil quantity can be changed over into gas amount (quantity) likewise and gas producers frequently refer to production as gas equivalency using the term.

E&P organizations report their oil and flammable gas reserve — the amount of oil and gas they own that is still in the ground — in similar bbl. and mcf terms. Reserves are many times used to esteem E&P companies and make predictions for their income and profit. Public oil and gas organizations are expected to unveil proven oil and gas reserve amounts as beneficial data, however not as a component of their financial report.

Obviously, new reserves are a fundamental wellspring of future income, so E&P companies invest a great deal of energy and money searching and exploring new undiscovered and untapped supplies or reservoirs. In the event that an E&P organization quits exploration, it will have just a limited measure of reserves and an exhausting amount of oil and gas. Income will definitely decline after some time. To put it plainly, E&P companies can keep up with or develop income by securing or tracking down new reserves.

What Is an Integrated Oil Company?

A coordinated oil company is engaged with at least two of the phases of oil production (e.g., both upstream and downstream). A considerable lot of the world's biggest and most influential oil companies today are integrated oil and gas companies, which have separate divisions for each stage. Being an integrated company takes into account unlimited complete control and efficiency. It also accommodates different floods of income and enhancement. In any case, because of the extremely high capital expenses associated with oil exploration and refining, boundaries to entry are exceptionally high for new competitors.

Oil Producing Countries 2023

Generally 50% of the world's countries produce oil in some limit. Oil creation is measured in barrels (as stated earlier) each day or BPD. Most oil delivering nations produce thousands, with their total output often limited by market forces rather than by production capability. For example, gas costs rose sharply because of the 2022 Russian attack on Ukraine, yet oil companies in the U.S. decided to take the increased per-gallon benefits instead of increment production (which would build supply and lower per-gallon prices).

- ***The United States***

With a good estimate of 11,567,000 barrels each day, the US is the top oil-producing country on the planet, as it has been for a long time. The US likewise consumes more oil than other nations around the world. As well as being the world's biggest oil producer, the US additionally imports as much as 8 million barrels of oil each day.

- ***Russia***

The world's largest country via land region, Russia is additionally one of its biggest oil producers. Russia supplies both oil and natural gas to numerous nations, especially China and Europe. This arrangement caused critical complications when Russia attacked Ukraine in 2022, setting off numerous nations in the EU and elsewhere to put a ban on Russian merchandise. Numerous nations, like Germany, carved out exceptions so they may as yet import Russian oil and gas, and yet looked to lay out new trading partners and energy processing abilities, in order to lessen their dependence on Russian exchange.

- ***Saudi Arabia***

The world's biggest exporter of oil, Saudi Arabia has around 15-17% of the world's petroleum reserves. Like most

Organization of Petroleum exporting countries (OPEC) nations, Saudi Arabia's economy is vigorously based on oil. The oil and gas industry makes up generally half of the nation's GDP (Gross domestic product) and 70% of its export income. Saudi Arabia likewise sends out natural gas, gold, iron ore, and copper.

- ***China***

China is positioned as the 6th biggest oil-producing nation, extracting around 3,838,000 barrels of oil each day. Remarkably, population size and the complete region of a country have practically nothing to do with oil producing volumes. More relevant factors are the country's mastery at exploring and extracting oil, as well as its political associations and the principles administering where it can and can't extract oil. For instance, the majority of the oil that China produces is separated from areas in the Middle Eastern nation of Iran, not the Chinese country. Throughout the long term, China has looked as its oil creation rates have gradually dropped.

- ***Kuwait***

The 9th biggest maker of oil is Kuwait. Not at all like many oil-production nations, had this Western Asian country encountered a serious drop in oil creation rates somewhere in the range of 2016 and 2020. In 2016, Kuwait determined 3,072,000 barrels each day of oil, contrasted with the pace of 2,753,000 BPD in 2020. This is ostensibly an unfortunate sign for Kuwait's economy, as oil makes up 60% of its Gross domestic product and simply more than 95% of its commodity income.

Chapter 2

AUTOMOBILES

Is it safe to say that you are prepared to embark on the exhilarating journey of launching off your own car business (automotive business)? With smart preparation, key navigation and creative thoughts, you can get it going. Whether you're building vehicles from scratch or assisting individuals with keeping up with their current vehicles, beginning an auto business is a splendid method for seeking after your entrepreneurial dreams and making something striking.

Beginning a car business is quite difficult. It requires huge capital, assets and information to find lasting success. Luckily, with the right direction and planning, launching off your own endeavor into the vehicles and trucks marketplace is not at all impossible

The automobile business has lots of business opportunities for anyone with interest.□ Assuming that you have been hoping to go into the area, this chapter will help you with having the right tips. Peruse on for more data on the best method to go about it.

1. *Decide on the area you want to specialize in*

There are several areas you can go into and a few examples include:

- Sale of accessories, which requires you to find good suppliers. you can go into franchising, where you limit your business to a well-established brand or be a general dealer, retailing for many brands.
- Mobile car wash business
- Tire sales and repairs
- Shuttle services and ride sharing
- Renting business and car hire

2. Carry out a proper market research

Doing your research is unquestionably significant while venturing into any business. Start by assessing the neighborhood market and understanding what you want to do in any other way to stand out. Take a search at the sorts of vehicles that different dealerships frequently convey, as well as their evaluating procedures. You ought to likewise consider expected suppliers and services accessible to you.

So suppose you need to open a Kia dealership in a specific region. A portion of the main activities are to see whether there is an interest for the items and administrations you intend to propose to clients in the territory and to do legitimate examinations to perceive how much rivalry there is.

A SWOT investigation will offer you a large part of the responses you really want. It takes a gander at qualities, shortcomings, open doors, and dangers. You get an establishment whereupon you will settle on any choices in regards to the business.

One more basic piece of statistical surveying is grasping your interest group. Would you like to target very good quality vehicle proprietors? Is it safe to say that you are hoping to give answers for center and low-class vehicle proprietors?

Concoct a profile or crowd persona for your objective clients. This will assist you with planning your deals and promoting technique in manners that focus on your favored client's best.

3. Come up with a business plan

Since you have every one of the experiences from your examination and research, the time has come to foster a Business strategy.□ Consider it as the methodology that will direct the entirety of your activities. It features objectives, timeline, game plans, and the monetary parts of the business.

While fostering and developing the field-tested strategy, it is pivotal to comprehend industry rules and guidelines. There are explicit rules you should comply with relying upon the line you take. Assuming you go into the showroom, for instance, it assists with realizing things like discharge principles.

Get the assistance of an expert legal counsellor to direct you through the process. It likewise doesn't damage to converse with others who have set up fruitful businesses in the area.

Conclude what sort of a company you need to set up. It very well may be a restricted (Ltd) company, association, or sole ownership. Figure out the implementation of each kind, particularly around things like tax collection. □ Once more, it assists with having master counsel on the most effective way forward.

Note:

In numerous countries, you'll require specific licenses and permits before you can sell or fix vehicles and trucks. For information on local requirements, consult your local government before jumping in to the business fully.

4. Decide on the location for your business

Searching for the right area for your business is significant to run a brick-and-mortar foundation. You can likewise go online, contingent upon the kind of business.

For certain, things like body shops, car wash centers, and service stations need a physical location. Others like tire and accessory deals can function admirably in the web-based (online) space.

There is likewise a third choice you can check out. Mobile service stations eliminate the expense of the customary physical location. In any case, you should put resources into a legitimate van with the right accessories. It ought to have the option to deal with the requests of steady movements as you serve your clients.

While searching for a physical location, take as much time as necessary to track down the right space. Your spending plan will determine where you set up your shop for business. You should likewise have adequate amounts to cover costs like rent, overhead, and other running expenses.

5. Raise capital for your business

A strategy will tell you how much financing need for the business. A few sources of capital are:

Your personal savings.

A credit from family or companions. It is fundamental to enter an agreement on how you will repay the loan. What's more, indeed, you should deal with your financing like any other credit. You would rather not lose family or companions on account of cash you didn't reimburse!

Apply for loans from financial institutions. It helps to have a decent credit rating while applying for credits. You get to appreciate better loan interests, permitting you to repay quicker.

6. Come up with a sound marketing strategy

On the off chance that you are entering an franchise agreement, you can leverage on the current brand reputation. But, if not, you will at first battle with brand awareness. It assists with setting aside some money for marketing and promotion. The good news is that digital marketing offers numerous low-cost options for businesses.

Begin by setting up a site. Your target audience will be curious about the business. They will no doubt utilize the search engines to track down you. Execute best Web optimization practices with the goal that the search engine can find you without any problem. Such practices incorporate using the right keywords, creating important and relevant content and streamlining your site for mobile guests.

Exploit nearby SEO by posting your business in the neighborhood registries. It is also essential to open an account on Google My Business.
Utilize entertainment platforms to get greater visibility.
Email advertising is effective and cheap. Begin by developing a target audience

list. Then, segment the audience for better targeting.

On various platforms like Twitter, Facebook groups, and LinkedIn, join relevant networking groups.

SUGGESTIONS:

Partnering with different organizations can pay off fundamentally by assisting you with getting leads, boosting deals, offer extra types of services, and that's only the tip of the iceberg. You ought to look into potential associations with auto vehicle parts supply, vehicle rental organizations, auto fix shops, and so on.

7. Hire Experienced Staff Members

At long last, it's fundamental to have experienced staff members who are knowledgeable about vehicles and trucks if you have any desire to convey magnificent customer service - from salesmen who can help clients in finding the ideal vehicle for them to mechanics who can assist with diagnosing issues rapidly.

"Starting an automotive business is difficult, but it can be done successfully with the right guidance." - Mariana Agular

With its natural simplified plan instruments, Designers assists business

visionaries with making proficient and
professional designs without having any
design experience whatsoever.

Chapters 3
REAL ESTATE

What is Real Estate?

Real Estate is defined as the land and any long-lasting (permanent structures) designs, similar to a home, or enhancements attached to the land, whether normal or man-made.

Real estate is a type of genuine property. It varies from individual property, which isn't forever appended to the land, like vehicles, boats, gems, furniture, and ranch hardware.

NOTE:

- Real Estate is viewed as genuine property that incorporates land and anything for all time joined to it or based on it, whether normal or man-made.

- There are five primary classifications of real estate which incorporate private (residential, business (commercial), industrial, crude land, and exceptional use.

- Putting resources into real estate incorporates buying a home, investment property, or land.

- Indirect investment in real estate can be made by means of REITs or through pooled real estate investment.

Understanding Real Estate

The terms land, real estate, and real property are frequently utilized reciprocally, however there are differentiations.

Land alludes to the earth's surface down to the focal point of the earth and up to the airspace above, including the trees, minerals, and water. The actual qualities of land incorporate its stability, indestructibility, and uniqueness, where each parcel of land contrasts topographically.

Real estate envelops the land, in addition to any permanent man-made augmentations, like houses and different structures. Any increases or changes to the land that influences the property's estimation are called an improvement.

Whenever land is improved, the total capital and work used to fabricate the improvement is address a sizable fixed investment. However a structure can be wrecked, enhancements like drainage, power, water and sewer frameworks will more often than not be permanent.

Real property incorporates the land and in addition to the freedoms intrinsic to its possession, ownership and use.

Real Estate Agent;

A realtor (Real Estate Agent) is an authorized professional who orchestrates a real estate exchanges, matching purchasers and venders (buyers and sellers) and going about as their delegates in talks and negotiations.

What Are the Types Real Estate

Residential real estate: Any property utilized for private purposes. Examples are single-family homes, apartment suites, cooperatives, duplexes, condos, and multifamily homes.

Commercial real estate: Any property utilized solely for business purposes, for examples, apartment complexes, Gas stations, supermarkets, emergency clinics, lodgings, workplaces, parking facilities, cafés, malls, stores, and theaters.

Industrial real estate: Any property utilized for manufacturing, creation, distribution, storage, and innovative work.

Land: undeveloped property, empty land, and agricultural lands like farms, plantations, ranches, and forest area.

Special purpose: Property utilized by the general population, like graveyards, government structures, libraries, parks, spots of love or even worship, and schools.

The Economics of Real Estate

Real estate is a basic driver of financial development in the U.S., and housing begins, the quantity of new private development projects at whatever month, delivered by the U.S. Census Bureau, is a critical financial pointer. The report incorporates building licenses, housing starts, and lodging completions information, for single-family homes, homes with 2-4 units, and multifamily structures with at least five units, for example, loft complexes1

Investors and experts watch out for lodging start in light of the fact that the numbers can give a general feeling of monetary and economic bearing. Additionally, the sorts of new lodging starts can give pieces of information about how the economy is creating.

Assuming lodging starts show less single-family and more multifamily starts, it could flag a looming supply lack for single-family homes, driving up home costs.

How to Invest in Real Estate

Probably the most well-known ways of putting resources into Real Estate incorporate homeownership, investment or rental properties, and house flipping. One type of real estate investor is a real estate wholesaler who gets a home with a merchant, then finds an interested party to buy it . Real estate wholesalers by and large find and contract properties yet do no remodels or increments.

The profit from investment in real estate are earned from income from lease or rents, and appreciation for the real estate value or worth. As indicated by ATTOM, which administers the country's premiere property database, the year-end 2021 U.S. home marketing chart shows that home dealers across the country realized a benefit of $94,092, a 45.3%return on investment , up 45% from $64,931 in 2020, and up 71% from $55,000 four years ago

Real Estate is decisively impacted by its location and factors, for example, employment rates, the neighborhood economy, crime percentages, transportation offices, school quality, civil administrations, and local charges can influence the worth of the land.

PROS AND CONS OF REAL ESTATE

PROS

- Offers consistent income
- Offers capital appreciation
- Enhances portfolio
- Can be purchased with leverage

CONS

- Is usually illiquid
- Affected by local factors
- Requires large initial capital expense

- May require dynamic management and skill

The shares exchange like some other security exchanged on a trade, for example, stocks and makes REITs extremely liquid and straightforward. Pay from REITs is acquired through profit installments and appreciation for the offers. Notwithstanding individual REITs, investors can trade in real estate common assets and real estate trade exchanged traded-funds (ETFs).

One more way for putting resources into land is by means of mortgage-backed securities (MBS), for example, through the Vanguard Home loan upheld through mortgage-backed securities

(VMBS), comprised of government organization supported MBS that have least pools of $1 billion and least development of one year.

Or on the other hand the iShares MBS ETF (MBB) which centers on fixed-rate contract mortgage securities and tracks the Bloomberg U.S. MBS List. Its possessions incorporate securities gave or ensured by government-supported undertakings like Fannie Mae and Freddie Mac.

What We Like:

- Liquidity
- Expansion
- Consistent profits

- Risk-changed returns

What We Don't Like:

- Not charge advantaged
- Likely to showcase risk
- High expenses

CHAPTER 4

HEALTH INDUSTRY

The medical and healthcare area is comprised of a wide range of ventures — from drugs (pharmaceuticals) and gadgets to health guarantors and clinics — and each has various elements. Investments in this area are impacted by numerous factors, including positive patterns connected with socioeconomics and negative patterns connected with reimbursement.

Medical sector management requires a complex way to deal with the fundamental drivers. Financial backers (investors) can benefit from interests in both the general sectors as well as its businesses. This part of the book will detail the distinctions among the different medical care businesses and which investors ought to follow prior to making a venture or investments.

Trends in the Healthcare Sector

While deciding on a medical sector to invest in, remember the following predominant trends and recent pattern. Changes to or continuations of these patterns can have suggestions for various areas in the medical field.

Positive trends include:

The aging population and the baby born boomers

Individuals living longer with chronic diseases and infection

Stoutness (obesity) and diabetes plagues

Mechanical (technological) advances

The worldwide reach of diseases and infections

Personalized medicine

Negative patterns include:

A single-payer framework (Federal health care/U.S. government)

The uninsured

Cost controls

Industrialism

Pharmaceuticals

Pharmaceutical and biotech organizations both produce "drugs", yet vary in how those drugs are made. Drugs are for the most part defined or explained as little chemical compound that effectively pass through barriers or membrane in the body, while biotech's are viewed as large protein compounds that experience difficulty going through membrane.

These organizations or companies frequently spend a critical percentage of income or revenue on innovative work (Research and development) to discover new mixtures (compounds). The "hit proportion" is exceptionally low as the disclosure of new mixtures or compounds is undeniably challenging and difficult.

While investing resources into drug organizations and companies, there are a few things to remember. You need to have some understanding about:

- The fundamental sickness or conditions that a particular medication treats
- The quantity of individuals affected
- The quantity of mixtures compounds presently accessible or available
- The course of discovery and coming to market, explicitly the

thorough clinical preliminaries required by the Food and Drug Administration (FDA)

- The accessibility of substitutes, including conventional renditions of drugs licenses.

- The general advertising and marketing system, which might incorporate income or benefit agreements with other different organizations and companies.

-

This is an industry that is significantly impacted by clinical-preliminary information, and the outcomes of the results of the information can influence the stock cost colossally. Positive shocks

— surprisingly good clinical information, quicker time to market, and so on — can make stocks value fundamentally in a brief time frame period, while negative surprises can make the contrary difference and effect.

Adding to that, post-retail information (i.e. aftermarket data), for example, the number of prescriptions written, market share, FDA alerts or the loss of a patent will influence and affect investments. This is an industry that requires dynamic and active monitoring on the side of the investor.

Who Covers and Pays the Bills?

Health insurers or guarantors are the organizations (companies) that take care of the bills - kind of. Organizations buy health care insurance in one of two general ways:

The buying company accepts the risk of covering every one of the bills.
The health insurer or guarantor accepts the gamble (risk).
An organization's decision can influence and affect its risk and productivity.

Underwriting skills drive health insurer's benefit. The better the endorsing, the lower the clinical costs comparative with the premium (or payment) received from the buying organization.

The key proportion that health insurers report is the clinical cost ratio. A trend analysis should be conducted on this ratio, which is comparable to the operating-profit ratio. Similar to the gross margin, but in reverse, the medical loss ratio is an important ratio (lower ratios are better). Additionally, since there are frequently timing mismatches between when medical services are used and when bills are paid, you want to make an investment in a company that has a conservative and dependable management.

Proper liability reserves is additionally a significant measure to survey. These stocks are by and large steadier and less susceptible when contrasted with drug stocks. Notwithstanding, following unofficial law, especially charges connected with Federal medical insurance and Medicaid financing, is significant as the U.S. government is the single biggest buyer of medical care services.

The House Ways and Means Committee is the part of the government that affects Medicare legislation.

Likewise, it is much of the time considered that the Democratic Party is more agreeable to medical organizations than the Republican Party, and stocks in the business will frequently respond to changes in party control of the public authority.

FACILITIES

The suppliers of clinical services — the medical clinics and facilities (hospitals)

— are the foundation of medical care in the U.S. U.S. regulations command that all offices and facilities with an emergency room treat anybody that strolls through the doors, whether or not that individual has health insurance or cash to pay for the services.

Free-standing clinics and specialty hospitals, which do not have emergency rooms and are therefore not required to provide services to everyone, have emerged as strong competitors to hospitals as a result of this legislation.

These facilities can single out which patients to treat and profit from higher payments from insurance agencies and companies.

In the meantime, hospitals' profitability is being negatively impacted by bad debt. The bad-debt ratio is an area of focus for investors. Additionally, cost management is essential to the profitability of hospitals. Numerous emergency clinic systems still can't seem to make technological advances like electronic clinical records, proper purchasing, and operating systems a part of their standard tasks, though this is by all accounts evolving.

Hospitals have a hard time keeping costs under control across multiple cost centers. The ones that do this well and use computer systems are usually regarded as having the best management. EBITDA per bed can also be increased by hospitals that are able to attract specialist physicians, such as neonatologists, because specialty medical practice typically receives higher payments for services.

Other important metrics include EBITDA per bed and overall utilization or capacity rates in addition to bad debt ratios.

OTHER INDUSTRIES

Pharmacy benefit managers (PBMs) are organizations that manage drug benefits for insurers. They work pair with the health insurer and can be viewed as a re-appropriated segment of health care insurance. By and large, when you go to the drug store to have a prescription filled, the drug store will contact (through PC) your PBM to check whether you are covered for the specific drug. Also, assuming that you accept your medications by means of mail, they as a rule come from the PBM's dispersion center.

PBMs will quite often profit from additional email exchanges and nonexclusive prescriptions filled in light of the fact that they for the most part get a higher margins for that sort of service.

Furthermore, PBMs get higher margins on specialty drugs, drugs that are infused, (for example, biotech drugs), or medications that should be refrigerated and are regularly not sold at a neighborhood drug store (in light of the fact that these sorts of medications or drugs require more attention). In this manner, PBMs that have an larger specialty drug store part will generally have higher edges.

Wholesalers or distributors are delegates or say intermediaries between the drug manufacturers and the drug stores (pharmacies), and get a help expense for controlling the coordinated operations for the drug organizations. Numerous merchants or distributors likewise have different lines of business that further develop margins, like packaging a portion of the medications, however the service-fee margin is a primary driver of benefits.

Medical technology and gadget companies manufacture a large group of clinical items, from bandages to artificial joints and heart stents. These organizations, like the drug manufacturers, spend an enormous percentage of incomes on Research and development, and some need to follow a similar clinical-preliminary way.

Putting resources into these organizations requires information and analysis of the new technology as well as the contenders and known substitutes. Reception rates and gross margins are significant marks of an organization's success, which is like other innovation (technology) companies.

CHAPTER 5

FOOD AND BEVERAGES

WHAT IS A FOOD INDUSTRY ETF?

A food-industry exchange-traded fund (ETF) is a food-focused fund that puts invest food-related organizations. This expansive industry covers family shopper staples, eateries, supermarkets, and food Circulation Company.

An ETF gives investors openness to a scope of organizations without the need to buy portions of stock independently. A food industry ETF is likewise a method for adding expansion to an investor's portfolio.

KEY Focus points

The food sector includes companies that produce and disperse food and drinks, liquor, and cigarettes.

A food-industry ETF is an exchange-traded fund that puts resources or invest in food-related companies.

Food-centered ETFs put resources into companies like eateries, food items, and shopper staples.

Understanding a Food Industry ETF

The food sector incorporates companies that produce and disperse food and refreshments, liquor, and cigarettes. Subsectors can run the range, including wheat and grains, sugar, espresso or coffee, and animals or livestock. Likewise included for the food business industry are U.S. fast-food chains with a worldwide presence.

Similarly as with other recorded ETFs, a food industry ETF may aim to match the investment execution and performance of a basic list. The Food and Agricultural Association of the United Nations tracks month to month changes in worldwide food costs. The FAO files order data on

food products like grain, meat, and
sugar.

Types of Food Industry ETFs

Consumer Staples: Food and drink
companies represent an enormous
shares of the holdings of consumer
staples ETFs. The top holdings of the
Vanguard Consumers Staples ETF
incorporate proctor and gamble, Costco,
and Walmart.

Food and Drink: The Primary Trust
NASDAQ Food and drink ETF
incorporates Coca-Cola, J&J snack foods
Corp., and the Campbell Soup Company.

Commodities: The future exchanging of commodities like sugar, coffee, and live dairy cattle are included for the Invesco DB Horticulture Fund.

Cafés and Restaurants: Fast food establishments as McDonalds, Chipotle, and Starbucks are exchanged the Advisor Shares Restaurant ETF.

How to Invest in Food ETFs

Investors might purchase individual stocks in the food sector. A food-centered ETF permits financial backers (investors) to hold shares in various organizations or companies across the business. Monetary or say financial institutions, for example, Fidelity or Vanguard offer record holders the chance to put resources into dynamic and active equity, fixed pay, or sector ETFs. These investments regularly don't need a minimum venture (i.e. investments) and are low in expenses.

What Things Are Viewed as Consumer Staples?

Day to day items used by consumers are viewed as staples and incorporate food and drinks (beverages), family merchandise (household goods), and liquor and tobacco. Consumer staples are things with predictable interest, no matter what the monetary or economic standpoint.

How Are Food ETFs Affected By Monetary (Economic) Turmoil?

Food-related ETFs assist with expanding a portfolio and can stay versatile in any event, during financial strife since consumer staples and food items stay in active demands during expansion, inflation, recession and downturn. Nonetheless, while food and drinks or beverage companies are seen as resistant to downturn, eateries or restaurants and their feasibility were tried during the Coronavirus pandemic.

Do Food Related ETFs Follow Food Records and Indexes?

A few records track food prices, including the Food and Agriculture Organization of the United Nations (FAO) Food Value List, which screens changes in the worldwide costs of globally-exchanged items and commodities.

Food-related ETFs generally track related records. The Invesco Food and Drink ETF depends on the Unique Food and Refreshment Index or Record.

The Principal Trust NASDAQ Food and Drink ETF imitates the NASDAQ U.S. Savvy Food and Drink Index or Record.

The food area includes organizations that produce and disseminate food and drinks (beverages), liquor, and cigarettes. ETFs open financial backers (investors) to a scope of organizations without the need to buy portions (shares) of stock. A food-centered ETF puts resources (i.e. invest) in food-related organizations like cafés, restaurants, wares or commodities, and consumer staples.

Industries That Can Make You A Millionaire

CHAPTER 6

MEDIA AND ENTERTAINMENT

The U.S. media and entertainment industry is the biggest on the planet, worth $717 billion, and has scaled to more than $825 billion by 2023.

The greater part of the media you see comes from one of the six significant media organizations, called "The big 6."

In 2018, the publishing industry in the United States, which includes both physical and digital books, made $38 billion.

We are without a doubt in a consumer culture in the U.S., and it's not only the actual items we buy every day that make us that way. The substance and content we appreciate is likewise a significant part of the product utilization and consumption process that we make, and it's all over. Simply on a relaxed drive not too far off, we can find eye-catching billboards for upcoming films and movies, new music playing on the radio, and promotions for computer games at the bus stop. Media is all over, and we as purchasers enjoy in the entertainment part of it.

The U.S. media and entertainment outlet is the biggest on the planet. The media and entertainment sector accounts for a third of the global industry and is worth $717 billion. The business incorporates movies, TV programs, advertisements, streaming contents, music and sound recording, broadcast, radio, book distributing, and computer games, and subordinate services or products. According to PriceWaterhouseCoopers' 2018-2023 Entertainment & Media Outlook, the industry was expected to be worth more than $825 billion by 2023 and it turned out to be more by 27%.

We see media and advertisements showing wherever in our day to day routine, however did you know 90% of the media you find in the U.S. come from one of these six significant media organizations: Comcast, The Walt Disney Company, News Enterprise, Time Warner, Viacom, and CBS? These six media organizations are known as "The 6."

With many media organizations in the U.S., we generally find it hard to relate the sub-organizations to their parent organizations. Indeed, twentieth Century Fox makes films and music, however shouldn't something be said about Fox Searchlight and Fox News — would they say they are a similar organization? The response is indeed, and they are completely possessed by the News Enterprise. Presently, Public makes it simple to separate the profiles of conglomerates by giving each organization's profiles, profit reports, and more in your grasp.

Portions of stock in these large media conglomerates and their procured organizations can trade for more than $200 per share.

As these organizations request a greater expense for share, certain individuals with low speculation spending plans might not have sufficient cash to deftly put resources into these organizations. This prompts the normal perception that only few of the wealthy can capitalize on long-term investments.

Fragmentary offers, otherwise known as cuts, change all of that. On account of cuts, financial backers (i.e. investors) can purchase stocks without buying the entire or whole shares. Presently, you can put resources into your dream companies and organizations with any dollar sum you have. For instance, in the event that an organization you like is trading at $100, yet you have just $20 to contribute, you could now purchase 20% (or 1/5) of a share of the organization. Should the cost of that stock ascent or rise and you choose to sell, you would procure a return with respect to your initial cut.

If you want to buy a stock that costs more than your budget allows, this is helpful.

Purchasing cuts of offers (shares) in various organizations can empower portfolio enhancement and diversification, and possibly bring down your portfolio risk exposure to one single stock. To put it another way, you no longer have to spend all of your money on just one share of a high-priced stock; instead, you can now buy cuts of one share from multiple stocks.

Purchasing cuts of offers in various stocks can assist with enhancing your ventures or investments and possibly diminish any major risks.

What are media and entertainment companies and organizations?

Some years back, the response would have been basic: movies and newspapers. In any case, presently almost all that you see or hear is viewed as media and additionally entertainment. There are heaps of subsectors in the business and beneath are large media and entertainment outlets and industries down into four subsectors.

Filmed Entertainment

This implies films, cinemas, T.V. subscriptions and electronic home video creation, and dispersion and utilization or consumption. Film industry receipts were supposed to outperform $11 billion of every 2019, including film promoting income of $991 million. This conventional sector of filmed entertainment has been significantly transformed by the widespread adoption of streaming services. The major players in this sector are adjusting to either develop their own services, like Disney+, or acquire smaller businesses that are already successful in this field.

Music

The music industry including touring and concert has increased to $22 billion in 2019. Beside actual music deals, all recorded music sections are up, including digital, streaming, and sync permitting (sync licensing). Sync permitting incorporates T.V. advertisements, in-flight entertainment, satellite radio, eateries, touring, live diversion, and product.

Book Publishing and Distribution

U.S. publishing, which incorporates both physical and computerized books, is the biggest on the planet, getting started at $38 billion of every 2018. Publishing & Distributing is estimated across three significant portions: professional, educational and customer publishing. Consumer books cover the biggest portion of the overall industry by a long shot, then the educational books and afterward professional's books. By 2025, digital publishing will represent almost 72% of all U.S. distributing.

Computer & Video Games

While gaming and Esports have their own unique spot in the business, they can be remembered for media and entertainment also. This sub-area was valued at $281 billion out of 2019, which is over two times its size in 2016.

Reasons Why People Invest In the Media and Entertainment?

The media and media outlet has encountered firsthand the gradually expanding effect and influences that technology has had on how individuals consume content. We are seeing a significant industry change from web based (streaming) to the internet of Things to shrewd home entertainment.

For sure digital, computerized, social, mobile and arising technology, for example, computer generated reality and computer based intelligence voice technology (AI), have ignited an obvious change in consumer behavior conduct, especially among the recent college grads. The attention economy is made up of these in combination.

How would you find media and Entertainment organizations to Invest In?

Research is everything! So before you make a plunge, it's useful to make a watch list of stocks and ETFs in the media and entertainment areas and become acclimated to the subject. On the Public application, you can begin with any stocks and ETFs that interest you, checking them as top picks without investing and watching out for them as a part of your every day or week after week schedule.

Following news and updates from organizations or companies and ETFs you are keen on can assist you with keeping up to date. By reading relevant market news every day, you can learn a lot about them. For every one of the very reasons that a major piece of being a decent essayist (writer) includes reading and perusing, being an incredible means studying and researching. When you're expanding your knowledge, it's helpful to learn, track, and stay engaged.

The primary concern

Putting resources (investing) into media and entertainment is a popular and famous path to seek after among numerous investors, however where to begin? Learn more about the sub-sectors by diving into them. There's a ton to take in. The industry has been a significant part of American life ever since its inception. Organizations in this industry are changing and developing to give the best content to consumers through technology advancement.

CHAPTER 7

TECHNOLOGY

The technology and innovation sector is an inevitably gigantic venture a potential open door for both corporate America and Wall Street. It is the biggest single fragment of the market, obscuring all others (counting the monetary area and the industrials area). More than anything, TECH organizations and companies are related with advancement, invention and creation. Investors expect impressive uses on innovative work by TECH organizations, yet additionally a constant flow of development filled by a pipeline of innovative new products, services, features and highlights.

Why the Tech Business Is Significant

These items, products and services are then spread all through the economy. There is no area of the cutting edge economy that technology doesn't contact and that doesn't depend upon the TECH sector to improve on quality, efficiency, or potentially benefit.

Tech is additionally eminent for its raging rivalry and rapid of date quality cycles. Albeit the models have been utilized so frequently they have become buzzword and cliche, it is in any case still a reality that PCs used to consume whole rooms, 16 GB of hard drive stockpiling was entirely sufficient for a tablet, and mobile phones used to flip open and closed. With that consistent drive to adjust and defeat contenders with new products, no organization can relax for long in the TECH area.

This quick pattern of outdated nature implies that victors and failures in TECH can't be guaranteed to keep up with those situations for a really long time. Microsoft was established in 1975 and in the wake of ruling in programming for PCs, has needed to play catch-up to speed in the mobile space. Similarly, Apple was left for dead during the 1990s yet sprang back to power with its innovative cell phone products. Besides, that dynamism and great development make technology a must-think about area for practically every equity investor.

Inside the gigantic and cumbersome universe of tech, it is feasible to see four key "super sector:" semiconductors, programming (software), systems networking, and hardware. While few out of every odd tech organization squeezes into one of these four uber areas, the greater part do, and it is a helpful method for discussing the area overall.

Programming (software)

Without programming, not a lot occurs in the cutting (modern) edge world. Programming is all over and is available in basic parts of everything from pacemakers to vehicles, yet none of those gadgets can do quite a bit of anything without programming. Thusly, it isn't is really to be expected that software is a tremendous industry too - on the order for many billions.

Programming isn't perceptibly repetitive by its own doing, aside from the more extensive financial cycles that overwhelm business. At the point when downturns show up, organizations ordinarily shorten their information technology (IT) spending plans and decrease programming purchases. In the meantime, the inverse is valid when recuperations start.

The product requires basically no infrastructure and is hard to safeguard by means of licenses or copyright to any compelling degree. Thusly, small new businesses with imaginative new products can show up basically overnight and with no advance notice. However a product supplier's reputation and capacity to offer help after the sale are serious variables and expected hindrances, this is by and by one of the most prolific classes for new organization or company development and new product presentations.

Cloud computing, for instance, permits a few organizations to offer programming as an on-demand application (regularly through the web or a closed network) instead of code really dwelling on a singular client's servers and hard drives. This "software as a service" has significant ramifications for the turn of events, development, dissemination, and usefulness of a multi-hundred-billion-dollar industry between programming suppliers and the end-user.

Networking & Internet

Networking, extraordinary and little, is apparently the greatest tech development since the microchip (CPU). The production of networks has fundamentally further developed effectiveness inside companies, however the internet (one enormous network) has worked with significant changes to trade and has supported completely new plans of action (business) like mobile banking and software as a service (SaaS). Networking is in many regards a sub-area of the other super areas; it requires hardware (which requires chips) and programming to work. All things considered, it is sufficiently huge and significant enough to stand all alone.

Investors can split their consideration between those organizations zeroing in on the customer (B2C, business-to-consumer) and those that focus on "in the background" business conducted between business (B2B, business-to-business). Much of the time, however, organizations like Amazon, Meta (previously Facebook), and Google obscure those lines.

For the second quarter of 2022, U.S. retail web based business alone was assessed to be valued at $257.3 billion a year in income and revenue, and that did exclude the worth from electronic assets transfer, information exchange, marketing, or online production network management.

Hardware

Hardware doesn't get the very measure of regard that it delighted earlier many years, yet it is as yet a critical piece of the TECH world. Albeit the software is progressively repeating the elements of many bits of hardware, there is as yet a significant market for some sorts of hardware and the area isn't quite as out of date as many accept. Broad-company and the internet just work as a result of a colossal spine of hardware, and programming is still at last a set of instructions; there must be a "something" to be told and to carry those instruction.

PCs have developed into a staggering cluster of gadgets from self-driving vehicles to cell phones that can basically duplicate and supplant a significant number of the functions of PCs. New thrilling products, for example, computer generated reality headsets and wearables can change consumer hardware, while the extreme client demand for information technology can fuel continuous development in switches, servers, and information storage gadgets.

Getting somewhat more unambiguous, hardware can be separated into many sub-areas, including communication gear, PCs and peripherals, networking equipment, specialized instruments, and buyer consumer gadgets. Tragically, investors might view a portion of these fragments as incomplete or deficient; do progressed electronic safeguard systems have a place in the customary aviation/defense class or category, or would they say they are TECH hardware? Investors shouldn't depend a lot on names while concluding what is or alternately isn't to be thought of as "hardware."

Semiconductors

Semiconductors underlie basically all the other things in TECH. The semiconductor business is an immense market all alone, however it is remembered to empower multiple times more in physical product that depend upon those semiconductors. Calculate each of different sorts of items or product and services that rely on semiconductors verifiably (what might programming at some point manage without a chip-using drone or smartwatch?), and it is seemingly the hub around which technology turns to.

There are various sorts and classifications of semiconductors. Chips can be partitioned into analog, digital and mixed-signals circuits, however it is more considered common to talk about contributes in terms of their definitive capability - like power management, microchips, microcontrollers, sensors, and speakers or amps.

In spite of the fact that semiconductors are universal, the business is exceptionally repetitive and follows a win fail pattern of ordering and capacity development. Regardless of that cyclicality, what makes the biggest difference for organizations in the semiconductor business is the capacity to design prevalent products (more elements per chip, less power utilization, greater unwavering quality, and so on) at the best cost.

What Investors Ought to Watch

One of the other fundamental bits of insight of equity is that tech stocks every now and again sport higher expenses than practically some other market class. In principle, this elevated degree of valuation is the acknowledgment of the above-average development rates that effective TECH organizations post. Practically speaking, however, even ineffective organizations can convey hearty valuations until the place where the market abandons those development possibilities.

Technology additionally has a better than expected number of public organizations that don't yet deliver benefits or income. The shortfall and absence of a history powers financial backers (investors) to use more mystery or guesswork while building limited and discounted income valuation models.

Financial backers (investors) can take a few consolation that exploration, research and steadiness (diligence) pay off in the tech area. Grasping and understanding an organization's product (particularly their benefits and detriments) and those of its opponents or competitors can deliver an investable edge. Obviously, this is a subtleties (sector and area) that those details matter.

Whether or not, investors ought to fret about valuations in the tech area is a subject of continuous discussion. Unquestionably, there are investors who have done well by following the development and putting resources into classification pioneers (or arising and emerging threats to the norm) and agilely moving from one organization to another regardless of valuation. Then again, investors who are not really agile, as they accept or misconstrue the opposition, wind up holding over the top expensive stocks with no support of significant worth to help them.

Conclusion

A few financial backers (investors) keep on remaining great clear of the whole TECH space and see it as invulnerable and nonsensical. Given the inescapability of TECH, notwithstanding, this is an essentially self-restricting perspective that removes one of the most unique and strong engines to current economies. A greater compromise, then, may be to just concentrate on cautious exploration and self-educations to invest where the valuations check out.